GEARED FOR GROWTH BIBLE STUDIES

FUTURE
AND HOPE

WHAT THE BIBLE'S ALL ABOUT

BIBLE STUDIES TO IMPACT THE LIVES
OF ORDINARY PEOPLE

The Word Worldwide

Written by C.M Potter

reaching the unreached

CHRISTIAN
FOCUS

Contents

PREFACE

**'Where there's LIFE there's GROWTH:
where there's GROWTH there's LIFE.'**

WHY GROW a study group?
Because as we study and share the Bible together we can:
- learn to combat loneliness, depression, staleness, frustration and other problems,
- get to understand and love one another,
- become responsive to the Holy Spirit's dealing and obedient to God's Word,

and that's **GROWTH.**

HOW do you **GROW** a study group?
- Just start by asking one friend to join you and then aim at expanding your group.
- Study the set portions daily, they are brief and easy: no catches.
- Meet once a week to discuss what you find.
- Befriend others, both Christians and non-Christians, and work away together.

see how it **GROWS.**

WHEN you GROW...
Things will happen at school, at home, at work, in your youth group, your student fellowship, women's meetings, midweek meetings, churches, communities and so on.

You'll be **REACHING THROUGH TEACHING.**

WHEN you PRAY...
Remember those involved in writing and production of the study courses: for missionaries and nationals working on the translations into many different languages. Pray for groups studying that each member will not only be enriched personally, but will be reaching out continually to involve others. Pray for group leaders and those who direct the studies locally, nationally and internationally.

WHEN you PAY...
Realise that all profits from sales of studies go to develop the ministry on our mission fields and beyond, pay translators and so on, and have the joy of knowing you are working together with them in the task.

INTRODUCTORY STUDY

A NOTE TO LEADERS

This is our answer to your request for a basic Bible study. The writer has produced this specially for those who have little knowledge of the Word of God and who need to develop a personal relationship with the God of the Word. However, even mature Christians will benefit from this study. We trust you will find it helpful.

The Geared for Growth Team.

ABOUT THE STUDIES

The Studies are divided into daily readings. Some need to be looked up in the Bible, others are written out. Each is based on a small section from the Bible, with questions which will help you understand it. The best way to do the study is to read the passage and answer the related questions each day. This will help you form a habit of daily Bible reading, and equip you to join the discussion in your weekly classes.

Keep your answers, and any questions you might have, in a notebook or folder. A Bible Atlas for finding places, and a dictionary for looking up words will also help you.

THE BIBLE

The Bible is a collection of sixty-six books. Originally, they were written on papyrus, leather or parchment scrolls, by many different writers over approximately 1500 years, concluding in about 95 AD. However, although human authors wrote the books, the true author was God. He inspired or 'breathed into' both the writers and the writings. This is what makes the Bible unique. It is not a creation of the human mind or experience, but is a revelation from God. The Bible tells us how this world came into being, and explains the existence of the human race. It helps us understand life's difficulties, and how we may face them with courage.

The Bible is divided into the **Old Testament** and the **New Testament.** Find them in your Bible.

Major themes of the Old Testament are creation, the entry of sin into the world, and God's preparations for a deliverer from sin. The New Testament was originally written in Greek and Aramaic. It is the story of God's deliverer - Jesus Christ, and of the total change He made in the lives of those who followed Him.

The writers of the Bible often quoted other Bible passages. They compared various texts and teachings, to make sure they understood the truth. We need to do the same. Important truths are repeated often. We also need to remember that Scripture must be interpreted 'in context'. This means we need to read a passage as a whole, not just as isolated verses. Most sects and cults spring from an overemphasis on one or two texts taken 'out of context'.

We could say that the Bible is like a vast and beautiful country of lofty mountain peaks, deep valleys, dense jungles and open meadows. In these studies, we can only glimpse the tops of the mountains. Exploring the whole country will be your lifelong adventure. May it lead you to love the LORD your God and His Word. Before you begin reading and studying the Bible, always ask God to help you understand it. In the First Letter to the Corinthians, chapter 2 we are told that God's truth is spiritual, and cannot be understood with merely human intelligence. No matter how clever we are, God needs to reveal spiritual truth to us.

At the front of your Bible is an index which will help you locate the various books.

Let us now look up some references and discuss the questions together. A 'reference' is like an address, telling you where to look in the Bible for the passage you want. The first verse in the Bible is *Genesis 1:1*, that is, the book of *Genesis, chapter 1, verse 1. Isaiah 40:8* means the book of *Isaiah, chapter 40, verse 8; 2 Timothy 3:16, 17* means the second book of *Timothy, chapter 3, verse 16 and verse 17. Jeremiah 29:11-13* means the book of *Jeremiah, chapter 29, verse 11 through to verse 13.*

1. *Isaiah 40:8.* What is another name for the Bible? How is it different from the material world around us?

2. *Romans 15:4.* Why was the Word of God written?

3. *2 Timothy 3:16, 17* ('Inspired' means 'breathed-out' by God, or produced by God.) What other name is given to the Bible? What makes it different from all other books? How does Scripture help us?

4. *1 Peter 2:2.* Why do we need to read the Word of God?

5. The book of Psalms is a collection of poetry and songs. In *Psalm 119*, the Word of God is referred to in almost every verse, and is called by many different names, for example 'law', 'testimonies' and 'precepts'. *Psalm 119:11.* As we memorise God's Word, what will it do for us?

6. *Psalm 119:18.* When God reveals spiritual truth, what do we see?

7. *Psalm 119:15, 16.* What happens when we spend time meditating on God's Word (regularly thinking about it)?

8. *Psalm 119:105.* What gives us clear direction in life?

9. In *2 Peter 1:20, 21,* we are told that the Old Testament prophecies were not originated by human authors. Prophets were 'moved' by the Holy Spirit (like a sailing ship borne along by the power of the wind) to express the mind of God, in words provided and ministered by-Him, in speech and writing. One of those prophets was Jeremiah. *Jeremiah 29:11-13.* What promises are given by God for people facing the uncertainties of the future?

10. What part do we have to play?

Biblical HOPE is more than wishful thinking. It is an attitude of confident, growing trust founded on God's nature and character, as revealed in His Word, and experienced in daily life.

In the following studies, we will discover that HOPE FOR THE FUTURE is based on certainties. The most important is the unchanging character of God, and the eternal nature of His Word.

You will gain more from these studies if you memorise a little of the Bible each week.

MEMORY VERSES: *Jeremiah 29:11, 13.*

STUDY 1
BY THE WORD OF GOD

QUESTIONS

Genesis, the first book of the Bible, is the 'Book of Beginnings'. You will remember that last week we saw the need to compare Bible passages and texts with other Bible passages, to make sure we understand the truth. We will now look at the beginning of Genesis, compare it with other related passages. Chapters one and two complement one another. Chapter two explains more fully, and with a different emphasis, information given in chapter one. This structure occurs throughout Genesis.

DAY 1 Day One of Creation. *Genesis 1:1, 2; Hebrews 11:3*
a) To be able to create the universe with no pre-existent material, what must God be?

Genesis 1:3-5
b) How was the light made?

DAY 2 Day Two of Creation. *Genesis 1:6-8; Hebrews 11:3*
a) How was the expanse of the sky made?

b) Consider the vastness of the universe. What does this tell us about God?

DAY 3 Day Three of Creation. *Genesis 1:9-13.*
a) What was made on the third day?

b) Which to you, is the most beautiful place on earth? How do you feel when you recall that it is God who created all that beauty? Choose a leaf from any plant, bush or tree; note its design, and remember that each plant can be identified by its leaves, for each is unique.

c) What would be needed to make such a vast variety, even among leaves?

DAY 4 Day Four of Creation. *Genesis 1:14-19.*
a) Light was spoken into existence on Day One of Creation. What happened on Day Four?

Day Five of Creation. *Genesis 1:20-23; Psalm 104:24*
b) What did God create on the fifth day?

Think of the countless species of fish and birds, the playful might of a whale, the songs of birds at dawn or the majestic flight of an eagle. Think too of how each living creature is made up of tiny atoms. Above all, think of the miracle of life which science cannot duplicate.
c) How would you describe God's ability to bring all this into being?

DAY 5 *Genesis 1:24-31; 5:1, 2.*
a) What groups of animals were made on the sixth day?

Genesis 1:26-30; Genesis 5:1, 2 In the Bible, the terms 'man' and 'mankind' are generic terms, referring to both male and female members of the human race.
b) What makes human life different from animal life?

c) What responsibility and honour did God give both Adam and Eve?

DAY 6 *Genesis 2:7.* We have seen that God planned, designed and created the universe. Before each step in the process, He stated what He was going to do, then created by His Word. We understand from this that God is a person, because marks of personality are widely held to include the ability to plan and design, create, and communicate through speech.

a) Is God like us in this, or are we like Him?

b) Man was made from the 'dust of the ground', that is, the soil and its minerals. What limitations do people have which God does not have?

DAY 7 *Genesis 1:31.*

a) What does the assessment which God gave creation tell us about God Himself?

b) Discussion: Since God created the universe, the earth, and the environment, is He part of it all or separate from it?

MEMORY VERSE: HEBREWS 11:3.

NOTES

What does the word 'God' mean to you? To some people, God is kind and generous- a bit like Santa Claus, handing out favours for good behaviour - but helpless in the face of tragedy. Others think of Him as a powerful figure of anger and vengeance. Still others think of Him as the spiritual force within nature. John 4:24 says that God is Spirit, but this is much more than a spiritual force. In our Bible Study we found that God communicates, creates, designs and evaluates. In other words, God is aware of Himself, and 'thinks' and 'acts'. These are the marks of personality. God is personal, not a mere 'Life Force' or abstract providence. He is neither an extension of the environment, nor a part of the cosmos - the spiritual and material universe. Because of these characteristics of God, we are not to worship the environment or any of its parts, thinking we are worshipping God.

God is the original living Person. He is not the creation of humans seeking religious experience. He existed before the creation of the universe, before time, as we measure it by the movement of the earth around the sun. He is so great that He spoke the universe into existence out of nothing.

Psalm 139, in poetic form, tells us that God is everywhere, and knows everything, even our thoughts before we think them. His intellect is far beyond human imagination, or comprehension. He is the ultimate source of all knowledge and all intelligence. Therefore we can say that God is not only personal, but infinite.

This infinite personal God is always reaching out to us, seeking to communicate, to help, lift up and renew. Have you thought that your circumstances and your future matter to God? Try using Psalm 8 as a prayer to talk to Him thoughtfully and quietly.

FOR EXTRA RESEARCH: Rule up a table like the following in your notebook. As you read your Bible, fill in everything you can discover about God. Appropriate readings in these studies will be underlined.

Place in the Bible	Bible Fact	What this tells me about God
Genesis 1: 1	God created the heavens	God existed before the universe came into being
Genesis 1: 1-3	His power and wisdom created the visible universe	God is all-powerful and infinitely wise
Genesis 1:31	God recognised creation	God is good

STUDY 2
"WHERE ARE YOU?"

QUESTIONS

DAY 1 *Genesis 2:1-3.*
a) Why was God able to rest?

Genesis 2:3, 15. (Fill in the missing words.)
b) From the beginning, God planned a balanced lifestyle for us,

consisting of six days .... and one day of ....
c) What does this say to our generation?

DAY 2 *Genesis 2:7-9, 15-17.*
a) What warning did God give Adam?

b) Was this warning to restrict or protect Adam?

Genesis 2:18-25.
c) In verses 18 and 20, what was God's purpose in creating Woman?

DAY 3 *Genesis 3:1-6.* (In Revelation 12:9 'the serpent' is identified as 'the Devil and Satan')
Answer TRUE(T) or FALSE(F):
1. The serpent cunningly planted doubts in Eve's mind about God and His Word (v. 1). (T/F)
2. Eve misquoted God (vs. 2, 3) by adding to what He had said in Genesis 2:17. (T/F)
3. By eating the fruit, Eve could become like God (vv. 4, 5). (T/F)
4. The serpent tricked Eve into thinking that evil was good, pleasant and desirable (v. 6). (T/F)

DAY 4 *Genesis 3:6.*
5. While the serpent was tempting Eve Adam was with his wife (T/F)
6. Eve did the right thing as a 'helper suitable' (Gen. 2:18 NIV) for 'Adam' by sharing the fruit with her husband. (T/F)
7. When Adam realised what was happening, he reminded Eve of God's command and refused to eat the fruit she gave him. (T/F)
8. *James 4:7 "Therefore submit to God. Resist the devil and he will flee from you."* If Adam and Eve had submitted to God, they could have resisted the serpent (devil) and he would have fled from them. (T/F)

DAY 5 *Genesis 3:7-13.*
a) As a result of their disobedience to God, what new emotions did Adam and Eve experience?

b) Whom did they blame?

DAY 6 *Genesis 3:21-24; Isaiah 59:2.*
a) To clothe Adam and Eve what did God need to do?

b) How did sin affect Adam and Eve's relationship with God?

DAY 7 *Genesis 3:16-20; Romans 8:22.*
a) How did sin affect i) human beings ii) the environment? *Romans 5:12.*

b) What do all people of the world have in common?

MEMORY VERSE: ISAIAH 59:1, 2.

NOTES

"Where are they who love thee for thyself? Where are they, those who love thee because they were created only to love thee? Where are they? Are there any on the face of the earth? If there are none, make some, for what use is the world if no one loves thee?" Archbishop Fenelon

Psalm 8:5 tells us that God made us 'a little lower than the angels'. Human beings are capable of amazing acts of love, creativity, discovery and technology because God made us 'in his own image', resembling His personality. At creation, God assessed man as 'very good', reflecting God's own goodness. Genesis 3:8 refers to Adam and Eve hearing the sound of the Lord God walking in the garden in the cool of the day. This suggests that the sound was familiar; that there had been regular times when God met and communicated with them, and they were comfortable in His presence.

Satan
However, a creature called by such names as the serpent, Satan, or the devil cunningly offered something Adam and Eve already had: likeness to God, while insinuating that God was depriving them of it! It was a blasphemous attack against God's integrity and truthfulness.

Adam and Eve
Being made in the image of God included self determination (the ability to make choices, or free will). Instead of using their self-determination to obey God and resist the devil, Adam and Eve recklessly accepted Satan's empty promise, rejected God's authority, and gave Satan the place that belonged only to God.

This rebellion against God is called sin. It separates us from God, and is the reason for the loneliness, the sense of orphanage, in the human heart. Due to our inherited sin, every aspect of the image of God within us is defaced and spoiled. Morally, we have a bent towards unrighteousness. Mentally, we are fallible, prone to errors and mistakes. Genuine freedom of the will was lost, so that it is easier to choose. the bad, rather than the good. None of us reach our full potential. All that we are and do falls short of what we could have been. The world around, declared 'good' by God, was also spoiled, subject to decay, disease and disaster.. Adam and Eve were alienated from God, each other and nature.

Nevertheless God came looking for them. The most poignant sound in history is God's call, "Where are you?" It can be heard today echoing through the Bible. God's search for us gives us hope.
Use Psalm 143 to talk to God.

STUDY 3
HOPE IN THE MIDST OF DESPAIR

QUESTIONS

DAY 1 *Genesis 3:14, 15.*

a) Fill in the blank spaces: Even in the midst of the despair of Eden, God promised that a deliverer would come, who would crush the head of God's enemy (Satan) fatally wounding him, but would suffer himself. The promise was veiled at first, but became clearer through time. *Genesis 4:1-5; Hebrews 11:4.*

b) Why was Abel's sacrifice accepted and Cain's rejected? *Genesis 4:6-17.*

c) The first human death was a tragedy, a dreadful consequence of God's warning of Genesis 2:17. How did God try to prevent it?

DAY 2 *Genesis 6:5-7, 12.*

a) What did God see in the mind and actions of man and what did He decide to do about it?

b) Which words emphasise this?

c) What does our society have in common with Noah's?

DAY 3 *Genesis 6:8-7:5; Hebrews 11: 7.*

a) What made Noah different from the people around him?

b) How did he and his family escape God's judgement?

DAY 4 *Genesis 11:1-9.*
   a) People quickly forgot the terrible lessons of the past. What were the two aims of the builders of Babel?

   b) Suggest reasons why God was not pleased with their efforts.

DAY 5 *Genesis 12:1-3.*
   As the world's population grew; God's plans for a deliverer focused on one man, Abram. This man's descendants would become a nation through which the deliverer would come. Abram lived in Ur, a well developed city with sophisticated buildings and a large library, devoted to gods other than God the creator.
   a) What command and what promises did God give Abram?

   Hebrews 11:8.
   b) What did Abram (Abraham) have in common with Noah?

DAY 6 *Genesis 17-1-8.*
   a) What command did Almighty God give in verse 1, and what promise in verse 4?

   Romans 4:18.
   b) What was the basis of Abraham's hope?

DAY 7 *Genesis 17:1-8; 21:1-7; Hebrews 11:1, 2.*
   a) What was so amazing about the birth of Isaac?

   b) What was the basis of Sarah's hope?

FOR PERSONAL REFLECTION: Am I trusting God and obeying Him?
MEMORY VERSE: Hebrews 11:6.

BLOOD SACRIFICE

When God killed animals to clothe Adam and Eve, he was revealing to them that blood must be shed to make amends for sin. This principle was later written into Hebrew law in Leviticus 17:11. Hebrews 11:4 says that *'Abel offered his sacrifice by faith;'* that is, trust in God and obedience to the principle he had revealed. Cain however, brought a sacrifice of self-effort, not faith, and God rejected it. God also warned Cain that sin was lurking in his heart waiting to pounce on him. Cain ignored the word of God. His unresolved anger festered into envy and hatred, which led to murder. Later, Cain was not sorry about his sin, but his punishment. His sin destroyed his brother, separated him from his parents, and forced him to become a wanderer. (By that time Adam and Eve would have had other children, so Cain would have married a relative, probably a sister, as laws against incest had not yet been given.) Hope was restored to Adam and Eve when God gave them another son, Seth, to carry on the godly line.

THE FLOOD

However, within ten generations, sin had so polluted the earth that only one man had faith in God. Noah heard his word, and believed what God said. His faith led to action, no doubt to the mockery of his neighbours! The account of the Flood is written into the history of many ancient peoples. Geological evidence of the Flood can be seen all over the earth, and is being continually gathered by qualified scientists.

Through the Flood, God demonstrated justice and mercy: mercy to Noah and the animal species, but judgement on human wickedness. The world had become so corrupt, violent and rebellious, that God, being perfectly just, could not allow such wickedness to continue. Similarly, God judged Babel, where, Nimrod founded a city on human might, the search for fame and notoriety, rebellion against God, and self-built religion.

In comparison with Nimrod and his descendants, Abraham was prepared to leave his idols and the comfort of the city to become a nomad, moving in response to God's command and promises. God said I will show you. I will make you. I will bless you. Abraham believed and obeyed.

It is not that faith is believing in spite of the evidence. Faith is obeying regardless of the consequences. The result of Abraham's obedience was a promise that the whole world would be blessed through him. The hope of Genesis 3:15 was passed down through him.

Suggestion for meditation: Psalm 1.

STUDY 4
GOD MEANT IT FOR GOOD

QUESTIONS

DAY 1 Last week we looked at the calling of Abraham and the birth of Isaac. Isaac's second son, Jacob, was a schemer and a cheat.
Genesis 32:24-30.
a) Despite all the flaws in his character, what was Jacob determined to have?

b) What new name did God give to Jacob (v. 28)?
(For more details on Isaac and Jacob, read Gen. 22:1-19; Gen. 24:1-67; Gen. 25:19-34; Gen. 27-35).

DAY 2 *Genesis 37:1-28.*
a) Why did Jacob (Israel) favour Joseph?

b) Why did Joseph's brothers sell him as a slave? (For more details on Joseph, read Gen. 39–44.).

DAY 3 *Genesis 41:17-32.*
Years later, Pharaoh the King of Egypt had a disturbing dream.
a) What interpretation did Joseph give of this dream?

Genesis 41:33-45.
b) Joseph was only a prisoner, but what did he have that prevented total disaster in the whole region?

DAY 4 *Genesis 45:1-11; Genesis 50:20.*
a) When Joseph's brothers came to Egypt to buy food, what did Joseph give as the reason for his suffering?

b) What did he provide for his family?

DAY 5 *Exodus 1:1-14.*
    a) Four hundred years later, the descendants of Jacob (Israel) were still in Egypt. Why did Pharaoh (the King of Egypt) treat the Israelites harshly?

    Exodus 1:15-22.
    b) What methods of population control did Pharaoh order?

DAY 6 *Exodus 2:1-25; Acts 7:21, 22.*
    a) Whose family adopted Moses?

    b) What were his strengths?

DAY 7 *Exodus 2:11-22; Acts 7:23-25.* Moses was apparently aware that he was an Israelite, and was sympathetic with the suffering of his people.
    a) How did he try to solve the peoples problems?

    b) What did his own people think of Moses?

FOR PERSONAL REFLECTION: Have there been painful circumstances in my life for which I need to forgive people and trust God to work for good?

MEMORY VERSE: GENESIS 50:20.

NOTES

The Old Testament is the outworking of 'the book of the genealogy of Adam' (Gen. 5:1). As it traces Adam's descendants and records the events of their lives, it is at times an unhappy and even ugly story. It reveals the consequences of sin, and the causes of suffering. It describes with graphic honesty the strengths and weaknesses of the Biblical characters.

However, in the face of the worst that Satan, sin and corrupt human nature can do, there is a recurring theme that lifts our hearts and brings us hope: "God meant it for good". This is carried over into the New Testament, and reaches its highest point in chapter eight of the book of Romans.

The life of Joseph, Abraham's great-grandson, shows how God works all things for good in the lives of those who love Him. Joseph was the beloved, pampered son of Jacob and his favourite wife Rachel. His brothers envied and hated Joseph, plotted against him, and sold him as a slave. Later, he suffered through unjust arrest and imprisonment; but through this suffering was promoted to the highest position in Egypt, next only to the King. By his wisdom and power, he saved his people from death by starvation.

During years of suffering, Joseph trusted God and served Him. In the face of temptation, Joseph put righteousness first. When power was given to him, he used it for others. Finally, when his brothers knelt at his feet, he forgave them and provided for them extravagantly.

God used Joseph to bring His people out of Canaan, not only to provide for them in famine, but to protect them from the evil lifestyle and wicked religious practices of the surrounding tribes. In Egypt, the Israelites (known as Hebrews) lived as a segregated tribe. Over the next four hundred years they multiplied from a family to a budding nation. To the Egyptians, this high fertility rate was a threat to national security. Their solution was to make slaves of the men and kill the baby boys.

Moses however, even in repression and infanticide, God was working for good. Ironically, one of the condemned Hebrew babes grew up instead, in Pharaoh's palace. Moses received a royal education that equipped him to later write the first five books of the Bible. One thing the impressive education did not supply was a trusting faith in the living God. Moses tried to rescue his people his way, with the weapons he had been trained to use as a Prince and soldier of Egypt. He spent the next forty years minding sheep in the desert.
Suggestion for prayer: Psalm 56.

STUDY 5
ON EAGLES' WINGS

QUESTIONS

DAY 1 Exodus 3:1-6.

a) Forty years later, Moses, the ex-prince, was still working for his father-in-law Jethro (or Ruel). What might he have learned through this experience?

b) In Eastern culture, removal of the footwear is a sign of respect. However Moses was being introduced to an idea, mentioned here for the first time in the Bible. Why was Moses told to remove his sandals?

DAY 2 Moses must have thought a lot about holiness for he later wrote "Who is like unto thee, O LORD, among the gods? Who is like unto thee, glorious in holiness, fearful in praises, doing wonders?" (Exod. 15:11). God is thus contrasted with false gods. Psalm 29:2 bids us 'worship the LORD in the beauty of holiness'. God's holiness reveals that God is 'other' than us. It elevates Him far above man, and He is the object of our awe and worship, Psalm 99:5. In Isaiah 40:25, we see that because God is holy, He has no equal, He stands in contrast to the whole of creation. Holiness is also the way in which God's moral perfection is expressed, Habakkuk 1:13.

a) Describe holiness in your own words.

DAY 3 Exodus 3:6, 14.

a) What names did God use to identify Himself?

('I AM' is the literal translation of a Hebrew word meaning 'the self-existent One', or the only self-existent being. He is the source of all other existence and life.).

Exodus 34:5-7.
b) How did God describe Himself in Exodus 34:5-7?

DAY 4 *Exodus 3:7-10.*
  a) What words show us that God understands human suffering? *Exodus 3:11; 4:14.*

  b) Last week we saw that Moses as a young man thought he would be the one to deliver his people. How had he changed in the intervening years? (For more details, read Exod. 4:18 to 11:10. They record Moses' conflict with Pharaoh, and God's judgement on the gods of Egypt through nine plagues.)

DAY 5 *Exodus 12:1-13, 29-31.*
  a) In readiness for the tenth plague, what was each Israelite household told to prepare and kill?

  b) What does the term 'Passover' mean?

DAY 6 (Exod. 14 records the Israelites' flight from Egypt and their miraculous crossing of the Red Sea on dry land, while the Egyptian army and its horses drowned). What forms of stealing does modern society accept? Exodus 19:1-6.
  a) To what did God liken His care of the Israelite people?

  b) What did He say was His purpose in delivering Israel from Egypt?

DAY 7 *Exodus 20:1-3; Deuteronomy 6:4, 5.*
a) What is worship and whom are we to worship?

Exodus 20:4-6; Deuteronomy 4:15-19.
b) What did God forbid and what right did He have to do this?

MEMORY VERSE: Deuteronomy 6:5.

NOTES

Personality is familiar to us - each individual has a unique personality. God's personality however has a peerless aspect which is so unfamiliar that we feel uncomfortable with it. It is called holiness. God's holiness sets the Lord apart from all other God's of religion or mythology (Exod. 15:11). We saw in Genesis that God is good. God's goodness is perfect, flawless, unique to Him, but sets a standard for all people. Its meaning includes moral uprightness and grace (mercy or loving kindness).

SET APART

Before Adam and Eve sinned they too were holy. 'Holy' in this sense, means 'separated from ordinary use and set apart for a sacred use.' They belonged to God, were secure in His love and comfortable in His holy presence. When they sinned, they hid from Him, embarrassed and afraid. In Isaiah 59:2 we learned *'your iniquities have separated you from your God, and your sins have hidden His face from you'*. Sin separated them from the holy God, as it still does, but Genesis 3:15 promised a deliverer to reconcile man to God.

The Lord's rescue plan focused on one nation. He commissioned Moses to lead a repressed tribe out of slavery in Egypt, into a special relationship with Him, as His holy people, *'set apart'* for Himself.

The gods of Egypt included the river Nile, the frog, the scarab beetle, the ram, the goat, the bull and the sun. Against all these gods, the Lord executed judgement (Exod. 12:12). In the tenth plague, the people of Israel were *set apart* **from** judgement by applying the blood of the Passover Lamb to their door frames. Obedient faith *separated* them *from* the Egyptians, to God.

After miraculously delivering Israel, God met them at mount Sinai to make a covenant. A covenant is like a business contract in that two sides agree to keep certain conditions and perform certain actions. God promised to bless Israel, and make them into a holy nation, *set apart* for Himself. They in turn, were to live appropriately, not yielding to the 'peer pressure' of surrounding wicked tribes, but as holy people. "Be ye holy as I am holy" (Lev. 20:7; 1 Peter 1:15, 16).

HOLINESS AND LOVE

We are either *separated from* God by sin, or *set apart* by God's holiness. Holiness expresses God's moral excellence in action. God's will is committed, His love self-sacrificing, His ethics pure and His justice impartial. High in the rocky crags of Mount Sinai, an eagle stirred its young for flight. As they took off on immature wings, they hovered beneath to catch them should they fall. This is God's analogy of Himself as He introduced the Covenant. He had rescued Israel on swift outstretched wings of holiness and love, to mould them into a people who would demonstrate these qualities to all nations.

Use Psalm 96 to think about the holiness of God.

STUDY 6
GOD'S STANDARD FOR LOVING MY NEIGHBOUR

QUESTIONS

DAY 1 *Exodus 20:7; 20:8-11; 31:13.*
a) Discuss ways in which God's name is 'taken in vain'.

b) Why did God appoint one day to be a day of rest?

DAY 2 *Exodus 20:12; Leviticus 19:32.*
a) By honouring parents and the elderly, to whom are we showing respect?

b) Why does respect for the elderly influence the future and prosperity of a nation?

DAY 3 *Exodus 20:13; Genesis 9:3, 6.*
a) What distinguishes human life from animal life, and makes it so valuable, that to deliberately take the life of another human is to forfeit the right to one's own life?

1 John 3:15
b) What causes murder?

DAY 4 *Exodus 20:14; Matthew 5:28 and 1 Corinthians 7:2.* In the Bible, adultery is when a married person has sex with someone other than their spouse. Premarital sex is called fornication. However, in Exodus 20:14, both forms of immorality are included.

a) Where does immorality start and how does the community encourage it?

b) What is the best way to prevent immorality?

DAY 5 *Exodus 20:15; Leviticus 19:13, 35; Romans 13:7, 8.*
a) What forms of stealing does modern society accept?

b) What is wrong with this?

DAY 6 *Exodus 20:16; 23:1-3; Deuteronomy 32:4.*
In what ways do we 'bear false witness against our neighbour'?

DAY 7 *Exodus 20:17; Colossians 3:5; 1 Timothy 6:6-10.*
Where does covetousness lead and how can we guard against it?

FOR DISCUSSION: Which is worse: to do wrong or be caught doing wrong?

FOR PERSONAL REFLECTION: James 2:10. Are there any commandments that I have failed to keep perfectly?

MEMORY VERSE: Matthew 22:39.

NOTES

TEN COMMANDMENTS

Most modern religious writings are founded on shapeless mysticism, but God's Covenant with Israel is structured truth, and truth is an essential characteristic of God. The Covenant includes a summary, the Ten Commandments, 'Decalogue' or 'Ten Words'. For three thousand years, the Decalogue has been an objective, absolute basis for ethical and moral standards, and shaped constitutional law in many nations.

Although mostly worded in a negative form (in protest against human evil), the 'Ten Words' set a standard for living a life of faith, love and hope. They can be read as promises, such as: if you will promise to be my people, I promise that you will be delivered from evil and alienation from God. Then you will love the Lord your God with all your heart, mind and strength. Out of this love will flow love for your neighbour. ALL people are our neighbours, for all are made in the image of God. Each person on earth has value, regardless of any distinction. We are to love them all as ourselves.

Summed up in Matthew 22:37, the first four Commandments comprise our duty to God. The second six, summed up in Matthew 22:39 comprise our duty to our neighbour.

Israel solemnly promised to obey (Exod. 19:8), but broke the first and second commandment even before God had finished delivering the details to Moses. Israel wanted visible, familiar, comfortable 'gods' like the gods of Egypt (Exod. 32:1). Throughout their history they repeatedly said they wanted to love and obey God, but failed in the doing.

The Commandments show us that we, too, fail. To begin with, who would have the arrogance to claim to love the Lord with all one's heart, soul and mind? We have all taken what does not belong to us. All of us have lied. All have envied other people, 'for *all have sinned and fall short of the glory of God'* Romans 3:23.

The Commandments show us firstly, God's standards; secondly, how far short of these standards we fall. In New Testament times, children of wealthy families were escorted to and from school by a trusted slave, a *'pedagogue'*. English Bibles use the word 'tutor' or 'schoolmaster' but the *pedagogue* was similar to a modem bodyguard. He guided the children along the right route, and protected them from harm. Galatians 3:24 says that the law is like a *pedagogue* whose task is to bring us safely to Christ.

Many people think they can earn a place in heaven by living by the Ten Commandments, but this is not their purpose. The Commandments protect us from rampant evil, and guide us to Jesus Christ.

Praise the LORD for His mercy by using: Psalm 103.

STUDY 7
WHO CAN THIS BE?

QUESTIONS

Prophecies about the coming deliverer are all through the Bible. The first was in Genesis 3:15. God prophesied that the deliverer would destroy the devil, but would be wounded in the process.

DAY 1 *Matthew 1:18-25; Isaiah 7:14.* Isaiah was a prophet who lived about 700 BC. The events which fulfilled this prophecy took place in about 4BC.
a) In what town was Jesus born?

b) Who was born in fulfilment of Isaiah's prophecy?

c) What does 'Immanuel' mean?

DAY 2 *Matthew 2:1-6; Micah 5:2 .*
a) Where did the prophet Micah, (who lived about 700 BC) say that the deliverer would be born?

b) Who was born there?

c) What astonishing statement did Micah make about him?

DAY 3 *John 1:1-3, 14-18.*
a) Who was 'The Word'? What was made through Him?

Matthew 3:13-17.
b) Who descended upon Jesus after John baptised Him?

c) What did the voice from heaven say?

DAY 4 *Matthew 4:1-11.*
a) In Genesis, Satan tempted Eve by making her doubt God's word and giving her false promises. What tactics does he use here?

b) What did Jesus use to defeat him?

DAY 5 *Luke 4:14-21.*
a) Isaiah 61:1-3 is quoted in Luke 4:14-21. List seven items in this prophecy which Jesus claimed to fulfil.

Luke 4:31-44.
b) Which of the prophecies are fulfilled even in these two passages in Luke?

DAY 6 *John 3:1-21.* Nicodemus was a member of the Sanhedrin, the great council of the Jews at Jerusalem. He came to see Jesus secretly, at night. The Sanhedrin had 71 members composed of the chief priests, prominent members of the high-priestly families, the elders and the scribes, who were the legal experts. The High Priest was the president. There were two main factions, the Pharisees who believed in resurrection of the body, and the Sadducees who did not. Under the Romans, the Sanhedrin had extensive powers, handling most government activities to do with the Jews, except the right of execution. Capital punishment required confirmation by the Roman governor.

a) What did Jesus tell Nicodemus about God's love and His plan for giving us eternal life?

John 8:58, 59.
b) In Study 5, Day 3, we saw that God identified Himself by the name 'I AM'. What did Jesus say about Himself that enraged the Jews so much that they wanted to stone Him to death for blasphemy?

DAY 7 *Matthew 8:23-27.*
a) What question did Jesus' disciples ask?

Matthew 17:1-9.
b) What did the voice from heaven say about Jesus?

FOR PERSONAL REFLECTION: How would you answer the question, "Who can this man be?"

MEMORY VERSE: John 3:16, 17.

NOTES

For the sake of time we have had to leave Moses and the new nation of Israel camped at the foot of Mount Sinai. After Moses died, God appointed Joshua to lead Israel into the promised land of Canaan. Later leaders included the great King David and the rugged fiery prophet Elijah. (You can read about David in the 1 and 2 Samuel, and Elijah in 1 Kings 17–19; 21; 2 Kings 1:2).

Moses and David were not only remarkable leaders, but also prophets. That is, God called them to discern events before they happened; and warned them of the meaning of those events. They spoke out against wickedness and injustice and were men of prayer. Moses and David were also outstanding authors. Moses wrote the first five books of the Old Testament. David wrote many of the Psalms. Throughout Israel's history, God raised up prophets who spoke God's words to the people, and wrote them down. They were the main authors of the Old Testament.

The message of a genuine prophet always came from God. It is only the false prophet who dares to take the office upon himself. The prophet's main task was to bring the word of God to his community. He warned them against sin, foretold judgement, and encouraged them to turn from sin and live as the holy people of God. Deuteronomy 11:1-5; 18:17-22. show that the true prophet was proved genuine in two ways. His prophecies were fulfilled, and he led people to follow and obey the clear commandments of the Lord, as delivered by Moses. The prophecies were given hundreds, or even thousands of years in advance. Their accuracy amazes the human mind; but it reminds us that because God is God, He knows all that will happen. He calls some people to discern this knowledge and bring His word to their friends, neighbours and community.

Prophecy is in sharp contrast to 'diviners' (or fortune tellers) and false prophets. In Deuteronomy 18:9-14 God condemns all such practices as abominations. God's people are to have nothing to do with them.

Beginning with Genesis 3:15, a common thread ran through all the prophetic messages - the coming of the deliverer. At first the prophecies were very general and veiled. Eventually they became clearer, predicting even the town where he would be born, and the way he would suffer to bring deliverance. Even more amazing than the fulfilment of these prophecies is the identity of the deliverer – the Son of God.

For meditation: Psalm 2.

STUDY 8
DESPISED AND REJECTED

QUESTIONS

DAY 1 *John 1:10, 11; Isaiah 53:3.* When Jesus came to the world which He had made, only a few understood who He was, and grasped the wonderful opportunities offered to them. How did the following people receive Him?
a) John 7:5 His half-brothers.

b) Matthew 13:53-58 The people in his home town.

c) Matthew 12:14 The Pharisees (religious leaders).

DAY 2 *Matthew 16:13-20.*
a) Who did the disciples think Jesus was?

Matthew 16:21; 20:17-19; Daniel 9:26. 'Christ' means 'Messiah' or 'anointed One'.
b) What did Jesus say would happen when He went to Jerusalem?

DAY 3 *Matthew 20:20-22; Mark 10:35.* The ambitious disciples, James and John, thought Jesus would soon set up His kingdom in Jerusalem.
a) What did they want?

b) What did they overlook?

DAY 4 *Matthew 21:1-11; Zechariah 9:9.* Kings usually rode horses, symbolic of victory and power. The poor rode donkeys, which were a symbol of peace and humility. Why did the people welcome Jesus so enthusiastically? What statement was Jesus making?

DAY 5 *Matthew 26:1-5, 14-16.*
a) What opportunity did
i) the religious leaders

ii) Judas, seek? This fulfilled a prophecy in Zechariah 11:12; *Matthew 26:6-13.*

b) The woman in Matthew 26:6-13 understood something everybody else missed. What opportunity did she take in spite of ridicule and harassment?

DAY 6 *Matthew 26:17-20, 26-30.*
a) In spite of the suffering which He knew lay ahead for Himself, what opportunity did Jesus take to prepare His disciples for the dreadful days that lay ahead of them? In Study 5, Day 5, we read Exodus 11:1-13 and learned about the Passover. 1 Corinthians 5:7; 1 Peter 1:18, 19.

b) Who is the ultimate Passover Lamb?

DAY 7 *Matthew 26:20-25.*
a) What warning did Jesus give Judas Iscariot?

Matthew 26:31-35.
b) What did Jesus prophesy the disciples would do?

FOR PERSONAL REFLECTION: Have I denied or rejected Jesus at any time?
MEMORY VERSE: Isaiah 53:3.

NOTES

Beginning with Moses, the Prophets told Israel that if they followed God they would be blessed. However, if they worshipped other gods or idols, they would suffer, be conquered by foreign armies, and taken away into captivity. Repeatedly, the latter prophecy was fulfilled.

In the time of Jesus, the Roman Empire ruled Israel. The Jews bitterly resented the Roman armies and officials who occupied their land; and the Romans mercilessly subdued any rebellion. Nevertheless, the hope of the Jewish nation lay in the promised Messiah. 'He will come', they thought, 'to deliver us from our conquerors and restore our nation to the glory which it knew under the great King David.'

SUFFERING MESSIAH

The writings of Moses and the prophets included the idea of a suffering Messiah, who would deliver man from sin. However, even the religious scholars and leaders, who constantly studied and taught the Scriptures, missed the point. The nation as a whole looked only for a victorious king.

When Jesus began His ministry, people were amazed by His miracles, His words and His authority. They were healed, fed, and some even raised from the dead. At the end of His three years of ministry, the crowds mobbed Jesus like a Superstar as He entered Jerusalem, King David's ancient seat of government. They expected Him to raise up an army and overthrow the Romans and missed the point when He rode in on a donkey. His disciples misunderstood too, though He had taught them for three years. Some were too busy squabbling about which government positions they would have when Jesus set up His Kingdom, to consider the prophecies of the suffering Messiah.

One disciple even volunteered for the darkest act in human history. Judas was Jesus' apostle, companion, eyewitness of His miracles, hearer of His sermons, and the group's trusted treasurer. To his fellow disciples, he gave no sign of what was in his heart. For the love of money he sold his Master for the going price of a slave, or about a third of a year's wage. Yet even to the last, Jesus warned him to repent.

We saw in Study 2, Day 6, that sin must be atoned for, by the shedding of blood. For thousands of years, animals were slain as a temporary covering of human sin. The time had come for the only atonement that could bring sinners into a right relationship with God, the death of the sinless Lamb of God.

For meditation: Isaiah 53.

STUDY 9
THE LAMB OF GOD

QUESTIONS

DAY 1 *Matthew 26:36-46; Luke 22:44; Hebrews 12:2.*
   a) Jesus knew He would soon die on the cross. What support did He ask for?

   b) How did Peter, James and John respond?

   c) Jesus was in such agony that He almost died in Gethsemane. How did He endure this distress?

DAY 2 Jesus' trial was a gross miscarriage of justice. Let us look at some of the evidence. On the next three days, insert appropriate Scripture verses in the blank spaces:
   Matthew 26:3-5; 27:1. (Find and write the verses down).
   1) There was a conspiracy to kill Jesus

   Matthew 26:...... ; 27:...... Matthew 26:57-61.
   2) Many false witnesses came forward, but their evidence

   did not agree *Matthew 26: ....* Deuteronomy 17:6.
   3) Finally two agreed, but misquoted a statement of Jesus (see John 2:19-22) referring to the resurrection of His body

   Matthew 26:......

DAY 3 *Matthew 26:3, 20, 40-47, 57-59; 27:1.* There were lawful times and places for meeting. The Sanhedrin could not meet at night, or in a private residence such as the High Priest's palace. The day began at six in the evening.
   4) Jesus' trial was at night *Matthew 26,.......* 27
   5) Jesus' trial was held in the High priest's palace

   Matthew 26: .... 26:62-68, 27:1, 2.

6) Jesus was forced to incriminate Himself under oath

Matthew 26: ....

7) The Sanhedrin could declare acquittal on the day of a trial, but could not condemn until the following day. Jesus was declared 'worthy of death' by the Sanhedrin, then taken to the governor early on the same day to have the verdict ratified.

Matthew 26: .... ; Matthew 27: ....

DAY 4 *Matthew 27:11-14. (Find the appropriate verses)*

8) The charge was subtly changed from blasphemy (claiming to be God) to sedition (claiming to be the King of the Jews, therefore

a threat to the Roman government) *Matthew 27:......*
Matthew 27:15-26.

9) Pilate knew the Jews' motive was envy *Matthew 27: ....*

10) Pilate and his wife knew that Jesus was innocent *Matthew 27: ....*

11) Yet Pilate refused the responsibility *Matthew 27: ....*

DAY 5 *Matthew 26:33, 34, 69-75.*

a) What warning did Peter forget until too late?

Matthew 26:50, 63, 67, 68; 27:11-14, 26-31.

b) How did Jesus react to abandonment, false accusation, insults and severe physical abuse?

DAY 6 *Matthew 27:39-44; Psalm 22:7, 8.*

a) Psalm 22, written by King David about 1000 years BC, was a prophetic Psalm about the suffering Messiah. Who mocked Jesus with these words?

Luke 23:34.

b) As Jesus hung on the cross, what did He ask God the Father to do?

DAY 7 *Luke 23:39-43.*
     a) What prompted Jesus' promise in verse 43?

     Matthew 27:45-50; Psalm 22:1; 2 Corinthians 5:21.
     b) What was Jesus made to be?

     c) Why did He let this happen?

Let us meditate on Psalm 22, bowing in awe and repentance at His feet.

Memory verse: Isaiah 53:5, 6.

NOTES

PERFECT SON OF GOD

Most of us think that if we found a perfect friend, we would love and admire that person, and be the better for it. We forget that when a perfect person was indeed on earth - the Son of God - He was hated and put to death. What had Jesus done that men should hate Him so much? He *'went about doing good and healing all who were oppressed'* (Acts 10:38). He was innocent, yet His enemies never rested until He was dead. *'They hated Christ because He was righteous and they were wicked.'*

The Sanhedrin, the ruling Council of the Jews, sent the Temple Guard to arrest Jesus secretly, at night. His shocked disciples scattered and disowned Him. The High Priest had already convened an illegal midnight trial with false witnesses on hand to convict Jesus. One notable witness was absent.

'If there was any living witness who could give evidence against our Lord Jesus Christ, Judas Iscariot was the man ... it was in his interest for his own character's sake to prove Jesus guilty.' The absence of Judas Iscariot at our Lord's trial is one among many proofs that the Lamb of God was without blemish, a sinless man.

Crucifixion was one of the most sadistic forms of execution devised by the depraved heart of man. It was invented in the dawn of history, and taken over by the Greeks and Romans for punishment of slaves. Death was very slow, sometimes taking as long as nine days. Soldiers stood on guard to prevent a rescue. The body weight strained agonisingly on the nailed hands and feet. Blood collected in the head causing a throbbing headache and fluid collected in the abdomen and chest. This was like drowning. The prophetic Psalm 22 describes in verses 14 and 15 the suffering of dislocated bones, weakness and thirst. It is said that every symptom of every affliction known to man was experienced in crucifixion.

However, for Jesus, far beyond the physical suffering, there was unimaginable spiritual horror. The holy Lamb of God was innocent. He had not ever sinned. Yet He became sin – our sin – the sin of the whole world through all of time – and died for it. In terrible supernatural darkness, Jesus took our place, experiencing the torment of being forsaken by God the Father. Then He voluntarily yielded up His spirit and died.

'But the real weight that bowed down the heart of Jesus was the weight of the sin of the world, which seems to have now pressed down upon Him with peculiar force: it was the burden of our guilt imputed to Him. How great that burden must have been, no heart of man can conceive!'

We must not think of this as something that happened a long time ago. Our sins made the bone-tipped scourge which tore the flesh off His back, and plaited the crown of thorns jammed onto His brow. Our rebellion stripped Him, mocked Him, drove the nails into His hands and feet. It was for our guilt that His blood was shed. The thought of all this should make us loathe sin, and turn from it forever.

Quotations are taken from Ryle, John Charles, *Expository Thoughts on the Gospels: St. Matthew and St. Mark,* (James Clarke and Co., 7 All Saints Passage, Cambridge, CB2 3LS) *'Matthew'* pp.387, 380, 362, 346.

STUDY 10

LIVING HOPE

QUESTIONS

DAY 1 *Matthew 27:50; John 19:28-30; Hebrews 2:14; Colossians 1:21, 22.*
'It is finished', from a Greek word that was commonly used in banking. It meant that the final payment had been made on a debt. What has the death of Jesus done for us?

DAY 2 *John 19:31-42; Mark 15:44, 45; Luke 23:50, 51.*
a) How do we know that Jesus was not just unconscious, but really died?

Nicodemus was the Pharisee in John 3 who came to see Jesus in secret. He and Joseph of Arimathea were members of the Sanhedrin and secret disciples of Jesus.
b) How did the trial and death of Jesus change them?

DAY 3 *Matthew 27:62-66.*
a) What did the Sanhedrin remember, and what did they do about it?

Matthew 28:4, 11-15.
b) What did the soldiers report to the Sanhedrin and what instructions were they given?

DAY 4 *Luke 24:1-8.*
a) What did the angels say had happened to Jesus and what did they tell the women to recall?

Luke 24:9-12.
b) Who thought the women's words were absurd and what had they forgotten?

X **DAY 5** *Luke 24:27-49; John 20:24-31.*
a) List the ways Jesus helped His disciples believe in the Resurrection.

b) Why are these details recorded?

DAY 6 *1 Corinthians 15:1-8.*
a) How do we know that Jesus really rose from the dead?

1 Corinthians 15:22, 50-57; 1 Peter 1:3.
b) As descendants of Adam, death is normal for all humans, but what difference does Jesus Christ make?

DAY 7 *Acts 1:1-11.*
a) List the promises and commands given to the disciples.

Romans 8:24-37; Hebrews 6:19.
b) How can we face tragedy, problems, disappointment, suffering or grief with courage and hope?

FOR REFLECTION:
What is my personal basis for hope, as I face the future?

Memory verse: 1 Peter 1:1.

NOTES

The resurrection of Jesus Christ from the dead was the most powerful action in history. Through it, Jesus Christ was proved to be God. Romans 1:3, 4 says *'Jesus Christ our Lord ... declared to be the Son of God with power, according to the Spirit of holiness, by the resurrection from the dead.' Jesus'* resurrection guarantees that all who believe in Him will also rise from the dead, to live eternally with Him.

Evidence for Jesus' resurrection includes:
i) The tomb was securely guarded, so the body could not have been stolen.
ii) Jesus' enemies did not ever produce His corpse.
iii) The disciples were not in the frame of mind to contrive a false resurrection. They were leaderless, grief stricken, confused and without hope; in hiding, afraid for their own safety. Even the Sanhedrin had more faith in the resurrection!
iv) Jesus could not have merely revived and shifted the huge stone from inside the tomb. His injuries were too severe, His body wrapped, and limbs bound.
v) The noise of any interference with the stone would have alerted the guard.

After His resurrection, Jesus met the disciples where they were, in their doubt and unbelief. Patiently He went to great pains to convince them that He had indeed risen. He explained again all the Old Testament Scriptures. At last they understood.

Jesus' resurrection, and later the outpouring of the Holy Spirit at Pentecost (Acts 2) changed them. They *'turned the world upside down' (Acts* 17:6), as they fearlessly proclaimed the great message of hope: Jesus' atonement for sin, and resurrection from the dead. As God changed them, so He can change us.

The New Testament was written by these people. Hope is a constant theme, combined with faith, love, joy and peace. As you continue your adventure of exploring the Bible, note all the references to hope. Look for the answers to matters raised, but not discussed in this study, due to limitations of space.

For meditation: Romans 8:24-39.

Biblical Hope is based on:
i) What God did in preparing for the coming of Christ into the world;
ii) What God did in atoning for sin through Christ;
iii) What God did in raising Christ from the dead;
iv) What God is now doing through Christ in the lives of countless people.
Biblical hope is not conditional on good or bad circumstances, possibilities or impossibilities. It rests in knowing that God is good, and will ultimately work all things for good, for those who love Him.

It does not make light of adversity, tragedy, grief, rejection, betrayal, pain, or suffering, but draws comfort and courage from knowing that Jesus experienced these and more. Biblical hope is like a mighty ship's anchor, embedded in the unseen depths of the sea. Chained to such an anchor, a ship can rise safely through screaming gales and pounding waves. Our hope is anchored in the secure, immovable depths of God (Hebrews 6:19).

"Now may the God of hope fill you with all joy and peace in believing, that you may abound in hope by the power of the Holy Spirit" Romans 15:13.

Hendricks, Howard G. and William D_ *Living By The Book*, Moody Press, Chicago, 1991.

McDowell, Josh, *Evidence That Demands a Verdict*, Campus Crusade for Christ, USA, 1972.

Ryle, John Charles, *Expository Thoughts on the Gospels: St. Matthew & St. Mark*, James Clark & Co., n.d.

Schaeffer, Francis A_ *Genesis in Space and Time*, Hodder and Stoughton, London, 1973.

Schaeffer, Francis A_ *The Great Evangelical Disaster*, Kingsway Publications, Eastbourne, 1985.

Sire, James W_ *The Universe Next Door, A Basic Worldview Catalogue*, IVP, 1988. *The New Bible Commentary*, Inter-Varsity Press, London, 1962.

The New Bible Dictionary, Inter-Varsity Press, London, 1962.

Vincent, Marvin. R_ *Word Studies in the New Testament*, Wm. B. Eerdmans Publishing Co., Grand Rapids, Michigan, USA, 1980.

Vine, W. E_ *An Expository Dictionary of New Testament Words with their Precise Meanings for English Readers*, Oliphants, 116 Baker Street, London WIM 213B, 1973.

Watson Thomas, *The Ten Commandments*, 1692, The Banner of Truth Trust, 1976.

Wiersbe, Warren W_ *With the Word: A Devotional Commentary*, Oliver Nelson, 1991.

Wuest, Kenneth S., *Wuest's Word Studies in the Greek New Testament*, Wm. B.Eerdmans Publishing Co., Grand Rapids, Michigan, USA, 1950.

ANSWER GUIDE

The following pages contain an answer guide. It is recommended that answers to the questions be attempted before turning to this guide. It is only a guide and the answers given should not be treated as exhaustive.

GUIDE TO INTRODUCTION

1. The Word of our God. It will last forever.
2. To teach us and give us hope.
3. Scripture. It is given by inspiration of God. It teaches truth; it reproves, corrects and trains us.
4. So that we will grow spiritually.
5. It keeps us from sinning against God.
6. Wonderful truths in God's Word.
7. We grow to love it.
8. God's Word.
9. God thinks peaceful thoughts about us, and plans a meaningful, hopeful future for us. When we call to Him, He will answer, and when we seek Him, we will find Him.
10. We must search for Him with all our hearts.

GUIDE TO STUDY 1

DAY 1 a) An almighty, all-powerful Creator so great that we are filled with amazement and awe.

b) It was spoken into existence by the Word of God.

*Note for **Leaders:** Biblical faith is not superstition, presumption or pretence, but trust in God, in His character, and in what He has said. It is belief in facts, not just an empty statement: 'I believe', or 'I have faith', but a statement with an object: "I believe in God, the Father almighty, Creator of heaven and earth" (The Apostles' Creed). The Trinity is evident in that Creation is the work of God the Father (v. 1), God the Holy Spirit (v. 2), and, God the Son, the Word of God (v. 3). See John 1:1-3; Hebrews 1:10; Colossians 1:16, 17. The word 'created' is used only in Genesis 1:1 (where God created out of nothing); 1:21 (where God created conscious life); 1:27; 5:1, 2 (where God created man, and the word is used repeatedly, indicating something special about the creation of man.*

DAY 2 a) It was spoken into existence by the Word of God.

b) He is infinite, unlimited, present everywhere.

DAY 3 a) The land, seas and vegetation.
b) Personal. Filled with awe, wonder, and breathless admiration.
c) Infinitely wonderful imaginative creativity.

DAY 4 a) The sun, moon and stars were made. Sea creatures and birds.
b) Creative Life so far beyond our imagination, and intelligence so vast most people cannot believe it.

DAY 5 a) Land animals, including creeping things (insects). God created man uniquely in His own image, i.e., beings resembling God in personality, with morality derived from God, dominion over creation bestowed by God, and the capacity for immortality. This is what gives each human person intrinsic value, and is the basis of human worth.
b) Dominion over the earth. They were to be God's co-regents, ruling the earth and caring for it wisely.

DAY 6 a) We are to be like Him, because man was made in God's image.
b) The human body is elated to the physical world and interdependent with it, physically and mentally limited and vulnerable. We need air, water, food, light and shelter for survival. Even the strong are helpless against the great forces of nature. We can only be at one place at a time. Although human collective knowledge appears vast, each individual only has limited knowledge; infinite discoveries are yet to be made. God is unlimited in space, time, power and knowledge.

DAY 7 a) God saw that everything He had made was very good. Therefore, to be able to recognise and identify with goodness, God Himself must be good.
b) He must be separate from it.

GUIDE TO STUDY 2

DAY 1 a) Because He had completed the work that He set out to do.
b) Work, rest.
c) Our generation suffers from high levels of stress and unemployment. Those who have work often have to work long and hard hours. Indolence or frenetic activity are equally unhealthy. We all need regular work and adequate rest.

DAY 2 a) Not to eat of the tree of the knowledge of good and evil.
b) To protect him from evil and death.
c) To make a helper for Adam who would be comparable, appropriate and suitable for him.

DAY 3   1. T; 2. T; 3. F; 4. T

DAY 4   5. T; 6. F; 7. F; 8. T

DAY 5   a) Shame, fear, guilt, defensiveness, blame-passing.
b) Adam blamed God and his wife. Eve blamed the devil.

DAY 6   a) He had to kill animals to use their skins.

Note to Leaders: God was teaching them that sin is so serious that blood must be shed to atone for it. 'Atone' means 'at one', 'to make one' or 'to bring those who are estranged into unity'. (Compare with Lev. 17:41 '...for it is the blood that makes atonement for the soul'). However this was not a complete atonement. It pointed thousands of years into the future, to the One who would atone for the sin of the whole world.

b) Adam, and Eve were separated from God by being thrust out of the Garden of Eden.

DAY 7   a) This was the beginning of:
i) human suffering, pain, interpersonal rivalry and marital conflict, stress, futility and frustration.
ii) degradation of the environment, violence, bloodshed and death among animals.
b) Sin and death.

GUIDE TO STUDY 3

DAY 1   a) Crush; the serpent.
b) Because Abel's sacrifice was offered in faith, that is, trusting obedience, and Cain's was not.
c) By i) urging Cain to do what was right, that is, to have faith in God and obey Him, and ii) warning him 'Sin lies at the door. And its desire is for you, but you should rule over it' (v. 7).

DAY 2   a) Wickedness, evil thoughts, corruption and violence. Judge the world with a flood.
b) Great (wickedness), every (intent of the thoughts of his heart), only (evil continually), sorry (grieved in His heart).
c) Wicked actions and thinking, corruption and violence.

DAY 3   a) Faith. Noah had a reverential fear of God, and obeyed Him in detail in building the ark.

b) He 'found grace in the eyes of the LORD'. God had mercy on Noah and warned him to build an ark to save his family and representatives of the animals from the coming judgement.

Note: Grace means mercy or loving kindness; Matthew 24:3, 7-39 and 2 Peter 2:5 parallel the flood of Noah's time with the second coming of Christ and the judgement at the end of the world.

DAY 4 a) To reach heaven through human effort (by building a temple-tower), and to seek fame and notoriety among their peers.
Note: Most probably, a shrine was to be set up on the tower for the worship of a heathen god.
b) Self-effort, pride and arrogance are sins which cut us off from God. We can only reach God and heaven through the way God provides.

DAY 5 a) God told him to leave his country, family and home, and go to a country which He would show him. He promised to make him a great nation and through him all nations of the earth would be blessed.
b) Faith (trust) in God. He obeyed God.

DAY 6 a) 'Walk before me and be blameless.' 'You shall be a father of many nations.'
b) God's promises.

DAY 7 a) Abraham... was one hundred years old and Sarah was ninety years old when Isaac, their first child, was born.
b) The faithfulness of God.

GUIDE TO STUDY 4

DAY 1 a) The blessing of God.
b) Israel.

DAY 2 a) Joseph was the eldest son of Jacob's favourite wife.
b) Joseph's brothers envied and hated him, particularly when he dreamed that the whole family would one day bow down before him.
Note: The coat Jacob made for Joseph signified that he was Jacob's heir, although he was the second youngest of the twelve sons. *Dreams were significant in the life of Joseph. Although he was spoiled, he was righteous and God-fearing. God was able to communicate with him, and chose him to preserve His people from famine.*

DAY 3 a) That there would be seven years of plenty followed by seven years of severe famine.
b) Joseph had wisdom and insight, which even Pharaoh recognised as the work of the Spirit of God within him.

DAY 4 a) God had purposed it for good, to preserve life - the lives of Joseph's family, and those of the people of the whole region.
b) All their immediate needs, and a safe fertile area of the Nile Delta in which to live.

DAY 5 a) They had multiplied so much that they seemed a threat to national security.
b) At the same time Pharaoh feared that they would 'go up out of the land', that is, Egypt would lose their slave labour.
c) Repression and infanticide.

DAY 6 a) Moses was adopted by Pharaoh's daughter.
Note: He was brought up in a royal residence, with all the training and pivileges of an Egyptian prince. This included reading, writing, copying of manuscripts, instruction in letter writing, administration and training in warfare.
b) Moses was 'mighty in words and deeds'.

DAY 7 a) He envisaged that God would use him to deliver his countrymen from the Egyptians. However he took matters into his own hands, doing what came as second nature as a trained soldier. It was an act of human force, fighting aggression with aggression.
b) They had no understanding of his vision, and resented his position and use of authority.

GUIDE TO STUDY 5

DAY 1 a) Humility and shepherding skills.
b) He was standing on holy ground, in the presence of the holy God.

DAY 2 a) God's holiness is glorious, awe-inspiring, beautiful, pure and morally perfect.
b) Holiness identifies Him as unique, with no equal, distinct from humans, or any part of creation.

DAY 3 a) The God of Abraham, Isaac and Jacob. I AM WHO I AM, that is, YAHWEH, the LORD or Jehovah.

Note: *The English word Jehovah is taken from the Hebrew word 'YH', a form of the verb 'to be'. It has the sense of 'I was, I am, and I will be'. For Moses, it was like an open cheque, promising him all he would need to bring the Israelites out of Egypt. To the Jews, the name YHWH was so holy that they wrote it without vowels, pronouncing it as 'Adonai' in reading Scripture aloud. This name 'presents God as a Person', and so brings Him into relationship with other, human, personalities. It brings God near to man ...in the Old Testament... the name is no mere label, but is significant of the real personality of him to whom it belongs.*

b) Merciful, gracious, long-suffering, and abounding in goodness and truth, being merciful when possible, but those who persist in wickedness will be brought to justice (2 Peter 3:3-13).

DAY 4 a) I have surely seen the oppression of my people and have heard their cry ...I know their sorrows... I have come down to deliver them.
b) The forty years shepherding in the desert had mellowed and humbled him. He was no longer brash and self-confident.

DAY 5 a) A male lamb in its first year, to be eaten with unleavened bread and bitter herbs signifying the years of bitter servitude.
b) On the night of judgement, God 'passed over' homes where the blood was painted on the door posts and lintels.

DAY 6 a) To an eagle taking care of its young as they are learning to fly. (See Notes, on study 5.)
b) To make them into a special treasure, unique on the earth, a kingdom of priests, and a holy nation.

DAY 7 a) To love with all our heart, soul and strength, that is, with our emotions, personality, will, and actions; reverential fear, adoring awe and wonder. The LORD God.
b) Idolatry. The worship of any naturally occurring or man-made object in the universe or on earth. He is the LORD God, in whose image we are all made, who made this world, and has dominion over the universe. *Note: Idols themselves are man-made, futile and helpless. (Isaiah 2:8; 40:18-20; 46:1, 2). But behind them is a demonic spiritual force which is a spiritual menace (1 Corinthians 8:4; 10:19, 20). Manley, G.T., The New Bible Dictionary, 'God, Names'.*

GUIDE TO STUDY 6

DAY 1   a) Through profane or careless use of God's name, inconsistency of life, claiming to belong to God but not living as a Christian, for example, using Christian bumper stickers on cars, but driving like the devil.

b) At Creation, God appointed one day in seven to honour His creative work, provide the human need for rest, allow time to spend with God, learn about Him and fellowship with other believers.

DAY 2   a) The LORD.

b) The elderly have insight, wisdom, knowledge and experience which are assets to their families and the whole community. Lack of respect for, and violent crime against the elderly indicates that the social structure is in peril. When the elderly live at risk, other vulnerable members of the community also live at risk.

DAY 3   a) Man is a spiritual being, made in God's image. Only God has the authority to terminate human life. *Note: Exodus 21:13 makes provision for excusable homicide;* Numbers 35:23 for accidental homicide and Numbers 22:2 for justifiable homicide; war was by the direct command or permission of God Deuteronomy 5:17.

b) Envy and hatred.

DAY 4   a) Looking lustfully at the opposite sex. Through inappropriate use of images of the human body, emphasis on immoral sex and acceptance of immoral sex in television, magazines, films, videos, advertisements, music, literature, etc.

b) Committed loving, faithful marriage.

DAY 5   a) Cheating, robbery, dishonesty; using other people's belongings without permission; employers not paying appropriate wages; dishonoured contracts; overcharging for goods or services; unpaid bills or taxes; undeclared goods at Customs checks.

b) Society's acceptance of stealing does not make it right. God's character is righteous and truthful. We are to reflect His righteousness and truth in total honesty.

DAY 6   Lying, gossip, slander, perjury.

DAY 7   It leads to envy, or desire for things or persons which belong to someone else, and can lead into every other type of sin. Focus on God's goodness and the good things we have, not what we do not have. Be thankful and content.

Being caught may FEEL worse, but the wrong is against God and/or our neighbour. Whether we are 'found out' or not, our actions will have consequences. In this world and its society we are accountable to one another, but at the Judgment Day, we will be accountable to God. (2 Cor. 5:10; Rev. 20:11, 12).

GUIDE TO STUDY 7

DAY 1 a) Jesus. (Jesus means 'saviour' and Jesus came to save His people from their sins.) ,
b) God with us.

DAY 2 a) In Bethlehem.
b) Jesus. (He was born there about 4 BC.)
c) That He had existed eternally.

DAY 3 a) Jesus, the only begotten Son of God. The whole of creation.
b) God the Holy Spirit.
c) 'This is my beloved Son, in whom I am well pleased.'

DAY 4 a) The same tactics: doubt, misquoting of God's Word, false promises and a seemingly easy way to gain power.
b) The Word of God.

DAY 5 a) 1.To preach good tidings to the poor. 2. To heal the broken hearted. 3. To proclaim spiritual liberty to the captives of the devil. 4. To proclaim that God's time had arrived to intervene in human history and judge sin. 5. To comfort and console all who grieve through sin and wickedness. 6. To give righteousness to those who mourn over their sin. 7. To glorify God.
b) Proclaiming God's time had arrived, preaching the good tidings, proclaiming spiritual liberty to those bound by the devil, healing.

DAY 6 a) He told him he had to be born again spiritually, by believing in (putting his faith and trust in) God's Son Jesus Christ.
b) He said He had existed before Abraham, (who lived about 2000 years before Christ). In other words, His existence was eternal. He also used the term 'I AM' about Himself, which the Jews recognised as a claim to being God. To them, this was blasphemy, which was punishable by stoning to death.

DAY 7 a) "Who can this be, that even the winds and the sea obey him?"
b) "This is my beloved Son, in whom I am well pleased. Hear him!"
Encourage group members to share what they think of Jesus.

GUIDE TO STUDY 8

DAY 1 a) They did not believe Him.
b) They were offended with Him.
c) They wanted to kill Him.

DAY 2 a) The Christ (the Messiah), the Son of the living God.
b) He would be betrayed to the Sanhedrin, condemned to death, delivered to the Gentiles (the non-Jews, the Romans), whipped and crucified. On the third day He would rise from he dead.

DAY 3 a) They wanted power and authority in Jesus' government.
Note: To 'sit at the right and left hand' was an expression indicating favour and power.
b) They overlooked Jesus' statements about His death, resurrection, and purposes to set up an eternal spiritual kingdom, not an earthly kingdom.

DAY 4 The people thought Jesus was riding into Jerusalem as a victorious King who would gather an army and throw out the Romans. Jesus was stating that He deserved their homage, but He was not coming in pride and power as a victorious political leader, but in meekness, identifying with the poor and the oppressed.

DAY 5 a) i)An opportunity to trap Jesus cunningly and kill Him. ii)An opportunity to betray Him.
b) She understood, at least in part, His statements that He would die in Jerusalem. She expressed her love while she had the opportunity, anointing Him with burial oils.

DAY 6 a) He celebrated a final Passover meal with them, in secret, so that they would not be disturbed. In celebrating the Passover with the disciples, He instituted the Lord's Supper, or Holy Communion.
b) Jesus Christ.

DAY 7 a) Judas would betray Him.
b) The other disciples would be offended, would forsake Jesus and be scattered. Peter would deny Him three times.

GUIDE TO STUDY 9

DAY 1 a) He asked them to support Him in prayer.
b) (Remember that James and John had asked for position and authority in the Kingdom, and Peter had vowed never to fail Jesus.) The disciples missed the opportunity to support Jesus in prayer, and help Him through His night of agony.
c) Through prayer, commitment to God the Father's plans and purposes, and His own commitment to gaining salvation for us.

DAY 2 (1) Matthew 26:3, 4; Matthew 27:1 (2) Matthew 26:59, 60;
(3) Matthew 26:60, 61.

DAY 3 (4) Matthew 26:20, 40, 43, 27: 1; (5) Matthew 26:3, 57, 58;
(6) Matthew 26:63; (7) Matthew 26:65, 66; 27:2.

DAY 4 (8) Matthew 27:11; (9) Matthew 27:18; (10) Matthew 27:19, 24;
(11) Matthew 27:24.

DAY 5 a) Jesus' warning that Peter would betray Him.
b) With silence and dignity.

DAY 6 a) The religious leaders quoting Psalm 22:7, 8, either forgetting its prophetic relation to the suffering Messiah, or using it in mockery.
b) Forgive them.

DAY 7 a) One thief admitted he was suffering justly, and placed trust in Jesus' Kingdom. Jesus promised him a place with Himself, that day.
b) Sin for us.
c) So that those who believe on Him might be made into the righteousness of God.

GUIDE TO STUDY 10

DAY 1 Paid in full the debt we could never pay; won a complete victory over Satan, whose head was crushed as had been prophesied in Genesis 3:15; earned our release from death, and the fear of death; reconciled us to God, so that we need no longer be separated from Him by sin, but may be holy, blameless, and above reproach in God's sight.

DAY 2 a) The soldier saw that He was dead, but to be sure, thrust a spear into His side.

Note to Leaders: The blood and water indicate He was dead. Even if not, His injuries were so great that without medical treatment, He would have died in the tomb. Pilate checked with the Centurion, who confirmed that Jesus had been dead for some time.

b) Joseph did not vote with the rest of the Sanhedrin for Jesus' death. Regardless of personal danger, he went to Pilate and asked for Jesus' body. Nicodemus helped provide expensive anointing oils and linen binding. After embalming the body and wrapping it in the linen, they laid it in Joseph's tomb.

DAY 3 a) That Jesus said He would rise from the dead. They asked the governor for guards and sealed the tomb.
Note: At the trial they used Jesus' statement about resurrection as evidence against Him. The tomb was probably sealed with clay, imprinted with the seal of the Sanhedrin, or a seal provided by the Romans; no one would dare break it. Roman soldiers were disciplined men. They would never have slept on duty – the penalty was death.
b) All that had happened. To say that the disciples had stolen the body.

DAY 4 a) "He is not here, but is risen!" "The Son of Man must be delivered into the hands of sinful men, and be crucified, and the third day rise again."
b) The apostles, the main disciples of Jesus. Jesus' words that He would rise from the dead.

DAY 5 a) Jesus explained the Scriptures, broke and blessed bread, ate, let them touch Him, and His scars.
b) That we may believe that Jesus is the Christ, the Son of God, and may have life through His name.

DAY 6 a) There were many eyewitnesses (all originally sceptical), including over five hundred believers at one time in one place, which excludes the possibility of hallucination.

DAY 7 a) Promises "You shall be baptised with the Holy Spirit" "You shall receive power when the Holy Spirit has come on you" "Jesus ... will so come in like manner as you saw him go into heaven" Commands "You shall be witnesses to me in Jerusalem, and in all Judea and Samaria, and to the end of the earth." Don't stand around waiting - get on with the job!
b) No suffering or distress can separate us from the Love of Christ. He is with us in everything. Therefore we can live as more than conquerors, in triumphant hope.

GEARED FOR GROWTH BIBLE STUDIES

Enable you to:

1. Have a daily encounter with God
2. Encourage you to apply the Word of God to everyday life
3. Help you to share your faith with others
4. They are straightforward, practical, non-controversial and inexpensive.

WEC INTERNATIONAL is involved in gospel outreach, church planting and discipleship training using every possible means including radio, literature, medical work, rural development schemes, correspondence courses and telephone counselling. Nearly two thousand workers are involved in their fields and sending bases.

Find out more from the following Website:
www.wec-int.org.uk

A full list of over 50 'Geared for Growth' studies can be obtained from:

UK GEARED FOR GROWTH COORDINATORS
John and Ann Edwards
8, Sidings Terrace, Skewen, Neath, West Glamorgan SA10 6RE
Email: rhysjohn.edwards@virgin.net
Tel. 01792 814994

UK Website: www.gearedforgrowth.co.uk

For information on Geared for Growth Bible Studies in other languages contact:

Word Worldwide International Coordinators
Kip and Doreen Wear
Tel. 01269 870842
Email: kip.wear@virgin.net

Christian Focus Publications
Publishes books for all ages

Our mission statement –
STAYING FAITHFUL
In dependence upon God we seek to help make His infallible word, the Bible, relevant. Our aim is to ensure that the Lord Jesus Christ is presented as the only hope to obtain forgiveness of sin, live a useful life and look forward to heaven with Him.
REACHING OUT
Christ's last command requires us to reach out to our world with His gospel. We seek to help fulfil that by publishing books that point people towards Jesus and help them to develop a Christ-like maturity. We aim to equip all levels of readers for life, work, ministry and mission.

Books in our adult range are published in three imprints.
Christian Focus contains popular works including biographies, commentaries, basic doctrine, and Christian living. Our children's books are published in this imprint.
Mentor focuses on books written at a level suitable for Bible College and seminary students, pastors, and other serious readers. The imprint includes commentaries, doctrinal studies, examination of current issues, and church history.
Christian Heritage contains classic writings from the past.

For details of our titles visit us on our website
www.christianfocus.com

ISBN 978-1-84550-411-3
Copyright © WEC International
Published in 2008
by
Christian Focus Publications,
Geanies House, Fearn, Ross-shire,
IV20 1TW, Scotland
and
WEC International,
Bulstrode, Oxford Road,Gerrards Cross, Bucks, SL9 8SZ

Cover design by Alister MacInnes
Printed by Bell & Bain, Glasgow

Scripture quotations are from the Holy Bible, New King James Version, Copyright 1982, Thomas Nelson, Inc.